HARD WORK,
BUT IT'S WORTH IT

The Life of
JIMMY CARTER

Written by Bethany Hegedus

Illustrated by Kyung Eun Han

BALZER + BRAY

An Imprint of HarperCollinsPublishers

Balzer + Bray is an imprint of HarperCollins Publishers.

Hard Work, but It's Worth It: The Life of Jimmy Carter
Text copyright © 2020 by Bethany Hegedus
Illustrations copyright © 2020 by Kyung Eun Han
All rights reserved. Manufactured in China.

ISBN 978-0-06-264378-0

The artist used Corel Painter to create the digital illustrations for this book.
Typography by Dana Fritts
19 20 21 22 23 SCP 10 9 8 7 6 5 4 3 2 1 ❖ First Edition

For Carmen Oliver, Kirsten Cappy, and Alexandra Penfold—
three women who do the hard work, day in and day out,
because it's worth it.

—B.H.

During the Great Depression, times were tough. But farm life had always been tough. There was work from sunup to sunset, no matter the time of year. From the very start, James Earl Carter Jr.—Jimmy— and hard work were fast friends.

At age five, Jimmy sold boiled peanuts from the family
farm on the streets of Plains, Georgia.

By age seven, he was spending long hours in the fields. He brought water to the workingmen, hauled firewood, and tended to the hogs and chickens. Jimmy's least favorite chore was killing boll weevils—"mopping cotton" was no easy job, but it saved the crop and got the cotton ready to sell.

Jimmy saw how hard work yielded strong results.

At least it did for some people.

In the 1930s, segregation—the system created by white politicians in 1896 that kept black folks and white folks from going to the same schools and churches or even eating at the same lunch counters— was the law of the land.

Thanks to life on the family farm, Jimmy knew more people of color than most white boys his age.

Rachel Clark took care of him during the long
hours his mother worked as a nurse.

And Bishop Johnson, head of the African
Methodist Episcopal Church, often dropped
by to speak with Jimmy's father. The Carters
would go to hear the bishop preach as well.
Then there was Alonzo "A.D." Davis,
Jimmy's very best friend.

Together, Jimmy and A.D. tromped through the fields, with Bozo, Jimmy's dog, nipping at their heels. Despite their close bond, the two lived in a world where Jimmy was favored just because he was white. Whenever they could afford it, the friends rode the train into Americus to see a movie. At the theater, Jimmy took a seat on the main floor or the first balcony. But A.D. had to climb to the third floor.

The friends wanted to sit together—but they knew it wasn't done. Not in Georgia. Not in the 1930s.

One day, when the boys were fourteen, A.D. reached a gate leading from the Carters' barn to the pasture first and insisted Jimmy go through before him. Was this a joke? Jimmy wondered. But it was no joke. The boys were coming of age, and A.D. did what he was ordered by law to do, letting a white boy, even his good friend, go before him.

Jimmy knew A.D. wasn't afraid of him but of any other white folks watching who might attack him for "not knowing his place." Nothing was the same after that. A.D. could no longer be himself around Jimmy.

None of it was right. None of it was fair.

Jimmy was beginning to understand how lopsided life could be, especially when it came to race and class. He wanted to do something about it. But what?

He wrote up a list of Good Mental Habits to help him navigate life's challenges—both inner and outer.

A list wasn't enough, but it was a start.

If you think in the right way, you will develop:

1. the habit of accomplishing what you attempt

2. the habit of expecting to like other people

3. the habit of deciding quickly what you'd like to do and d

4. the habit of sticking to it

5. the habit of welcomi

6. a person wh

shou

Jimmy's list carried him through high school and college.
And when he joined the navy, he and his wife, Rosalynn,
traveled far from the peanut fields of Georgia.

But when his father died, Jimmy,
who now had a family of his own,
returned to the racially divided South
to take over the family farm.

Once home, as a white business owner, Jimmy was expected to join the White Citizens' Council, a group that opposed black students and white students attending the same schools. When he refused, the Carter family business was boycotted by powerful whites.

Jimmy wouldn't stay silent anymore—he would not accept the ways of the South as he had when he was a boy. He owed it to himself. He owed it to A.D.

Jimmy didn't know it yet, but his career as a politician had begun. Within several years, he went from serving on the local school board to winning a seat in the Georgia state senate.

Next, Jimmy ran for governor of Georgia. He lost the race, but he didn't give up. In 1970, he ran again. This time he won.

Outside the state capitol, he addressed his constituents. "I say to you quite frankly the time for racial discrimination is over."

After all, it was only right. It was only fair.

Governor of Georgia was a four-year position. Folks asked—what's next?

Jimmy turned to prayer. What was next would be an enormous undertaking. Jimmy Carter would run for president, serving all Americans.

In his first national election campaign, Jimmy Carter and his team stayed with fifty-one families—of all different races—all over the country. He worked hard to spread the message that he was "a Leader, for a Change." And when the results came in, Jimmy had beaten the incumbent, Gerald Ford! He had won the election—fair and square.

Serving as president was the toughest job Jimmy would ever have.
Race relations were still a struggle. And all over the world people
were fighting—about oil, about religion.

President Carter sat down with the leaders of Egypt and Israel, men
who were considered each other's enemies, and asked them to consider
peace. They did.

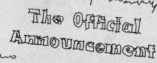

The challenges kept coming: An energy crisis. Bad press over the Panama Canal. But the biggest challenge of all came when more than sixty Americans were taken hostage in Tehran, Iran.

With his sleeves rolled up and his heels dug in, President Carter tried his best to bring all the men and women home. Despite his hard work—and possibly because of his conviction not to go to war—President Carter wasn't able to secure the hostages' release.

Though Carter ran for a second term, he was not reelected.

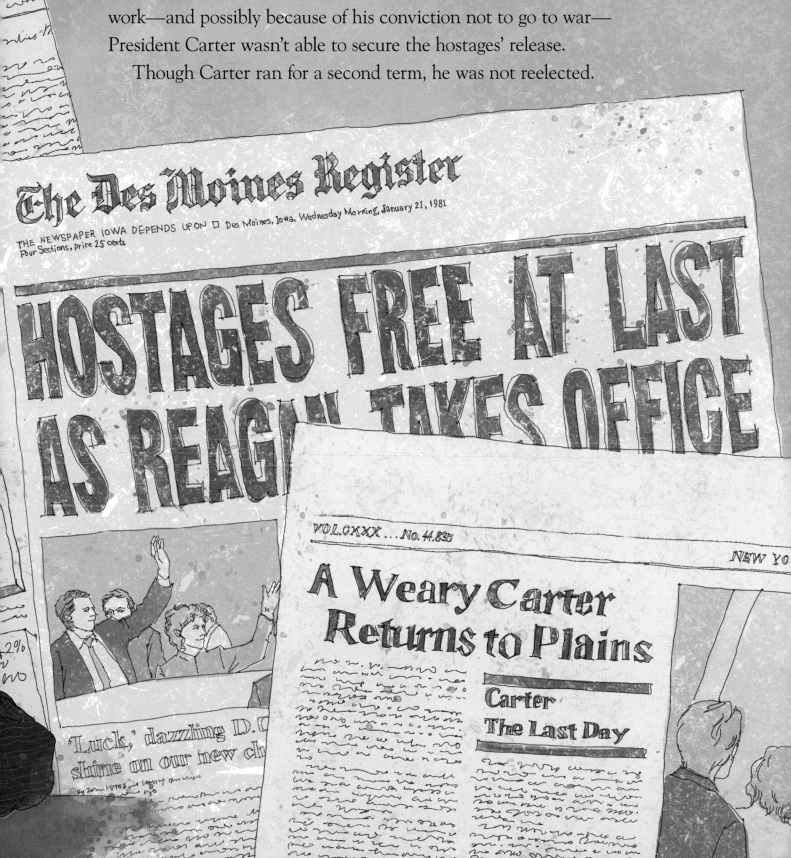

The Des Moines Register

THE NEWSPAPER IOWA DEPENDS UPON □ Des Moines, Iowa, Wednesday Morning, January 21, 1981
Four Sections, Price 25 cents

HOSTAGES FREE AT LAST AS REAGAN TAKES OFFICE

'Luck,' dazzling D.C.
shine on our new ch...

VOL. CXXX ... No. 44,835

NEW YO

A Weary Carter Returns to Plains

Carter
The Last Day

Just because he was no longer president didn't mean Jimmy Carter's job was done. He still lived by his list of Good Mental Habits. And he still wanted to help create a lasting peace. But how?

Back in Georgia, Jimmy and Rosalynn created the Carter Center, whose mission was "Waging Peace. Fighting Disease. Building Hope"—for people all over the world.

They picked up shovels and donned hard hats, volunteering for Habitat for Humanity, helping to build homes for the poor from the ground up. Thousands joined them.

And just as he did when he was a boy, Jimmy bent over his desk and wrote. Instead of lists, now he wrote books. And he kept fighting for causes he believed in—mental health care, clean water, equal pay for women.

Jimmy didn't know it yet, but he had a new career: humanitarian.

Jimmy didn't work for rewards or prizes, but in 2002 he was awarded an important one: the Nobel Peace Prize, "for his decades of untiring effort to find peaceful solutions to international conflicts, to advance democracy and human rights. . . ."

Now in his nineties, even after battling brain cancer,
Jimmy still works from sunup to sunset.
His efforts to build a lasting peace continue.
It's hard work, but it's worth it.

AUTHOR'S NOTE

When Jimmy Carter was elected our nation's president, I was five years old. When he left office, I was nine—the same age his daughter, Amy, was when the Carter family moved into the White House. I remember watching the news with my father—hearing about the energy crisis and the Camp David Accords and the taking of the American hostages in Tehran. It was a scary time—just as it can be today—but I felt secure whenever I heard the president speak. Later, when my family moved to Augusta, Georgia, I felt even more of a bond with our thirty-ninth president.

Jimmy Carter's childhood was filled with the makings of the man he became. Despite growing up at the height of segregation, Jimmy saw his parents cross the rural South's strict color lines: his mother, in her work as a nurse, serving the entire community, not just the white community, and his father in less direct ways, such as taking the family to see Bishop Johnson preach in the African Methodist Episcopal Church across town. Of Bishop Johnson, Jimmy wrote, "He was the richest and most prominent citizen of our community." Jimmy also felt great love for Rachel Clark, the woman who helped look after him and his siblings, and the loss of his friendship with A.D. marked the end of Jimmy's childhood.

Once Jimmy ended his navy career and returned to Plains with his family, he began speaking out against the Jim Crow laws he had kept silent about in childhood. Soon, Jimmy found more ways he could make a difference. His political career began small, on the local school board, but before long he was governor of Georgia. As governor, Jimmy Carter increased the number of African American staff members in the Georgia government by 25 percent. When there was racial unrest in Hancock County, instead of sending in the National Guard, Governor Carter sent in an adviser, a state patrolman, and a conflict expert—two white men and one black man. No bullets were fired and no lives were lost.

As president, Carter urged US citizens to conserve energy. He and his wife, Rosalynn, wore long underwear in the winter and refused to turn on the White House air-conditioning in the summer even when the temperatures inside hit over a hundred degrees. He ordered all 325 television sets and 250 radios unplugged when not in use. He asked the country to do the same.

In the fall of 1979, Iranian students took over their government, and on November 4, the United States embassy in Tehran was stormed. Sixty-six Americans were held hostage—and the hostage takers said they would not release them until their demand that the shah be returned to Iran was met. President Carter wanted the hostages released without going to war, and though he worked tirelessly to see this done, the hostages were not released until after Ronald Reagan was sworn in as the new commander in chief.

Many politicians would have seen this as the end of their careers—but not former president Carter. After his years in the White House, his true work began— that of a humanitarian. In 2002, Jimmy Carter became the second Georgian to be awarded the Nobel Peace Prize. The first was Dr. Martin Luther King Jr., whose picture Jimmy had hung in the Georgia capitol when he was governor thirty-eight years earlier.

Now in his nineties, Carter continues to heed the words he wrote in the eighth grade, in a list of Good Mental Habits he took down in a notebook: to "give up worry and anger; hatred and envy" and to "neither fear nor be ashamed of anything that is honest and purposeful."

Jimmy Carter is a hero of mine. I hope he is now one of yours, too.

TIMELINE

1924 October 1: James Earl Carter Jr. is born in Plains, Georgia—the first American president to be born in a hospital.

1928 The Carters move from Plains to a 360-acre peanut farm in Archery, four miles away.

1930 Jimmy attends Plains Elementary School.

1941 Jimmy graduates from high school. He then attends Georgia Southwestern College.

1942 Jimmy transfers to the Georgia Institute of Technology in Atlanta, Georgia.

1943 Jimmy attends the United States Naval Academy in Annapolis, Maryland.

1946 July 7: Jimmy Carter and Rosalynn Smith marry.

He receives a naval commission and the couple moves to Norfolk, Virginia.

1947 Jimmy and Rosalynn's first son, John William, known as Jack, is born in Virginia.

1949 Jimmy is stationed at Pearl Harbor, Hawaii. Rosalynn and Jack join him.

1950 Jimmy and Rosalynn's second son, James Earl III, known as Chip, is born in Hawaii.

1952 Jimmy and Rosalynn's third child, Donnel Jeffrey, known as Jeff, is born in Connecticut.

1953 Jimmy Carter's father dies of pancreatic cancer. Jimmy gets an honorable discharge from the navy and moves his family to Georgia to take over his father's business.

1954 The landmark case of *Brown v. Board of Education* is decided by the Supreme Court, which rules that separate is not equal and calls for an end to school segregation.

Jimmy is asked by the police chief and the railroad station agent, the leaders of the White Citizens' Council, to join those opposed to integration. Jimmy, even when his membership is paid for, refuses to join.

1956 Jimmy runs for and wins a seat on the local school board.

1962 October 16: Jimmy loses the primary for state senator but hears talk of threats made at the polls. He asks for a recount.

November 2: The recount committee rules in Jimmy's favor. A new primary election is granted. Jimmy wins by 831 votes.

1963 January 14: Jimmy Carter is sworn in as a Georgia state senator.

1964 July: Congress passes the Civil Rights Act, which outlaws discrimination based on "race, color, religion, sex, or national origin."

1966 Spring: Jimmy's mother, Lillian, joins the Peace Corps at the age of sixty-eight.

September 15: Jimmy runs for governor of Georgia and loses.

1967 October 19: Jimmy's only daughter, Amy Lynn, is born in Plains, Georgia.

1968 April 4: Dr. Martin Luther King Jr. is assassinated.

1970 November 3: Jimmy wins the race for governor of Georgia, beating Republican Hal Suit. Segregationist Lester Maddox is elected lieutenant governor.

1971 January 12: Jimmy is sworn in as Georgia's governor and in his inaugural address declares "the time for racial discrimination is over."

May 31: Jimmy Carter appears on the cover of *Time* as the voice and face of the "New South."

1974 December 12: Jimmy announces he will run for president.

1976 November 2: Jimmy Carter beats Gerald Ford in the race for the presidency, winning 40.8 million votes to Ford's 39.1 million votes and an electoral college vote of 297 to 240.

1977 January 20: Jimmy and his wife, Rosalynn, walk down Pennsylvania Avenue on their way to the inauguration. In his speech, Jimmy asks for a "lasting peace." He is the thirty-ninth president of the United States.

Jimmy signs the Panama Canal treaties, works on an energy proposal, and develops a weapons agreement with the Soviet Union.

1978 Jimmy invites the leaders of Israel and Egypt to Camp David to develop a peace plan. This is known as the Camp David Accords. He signs the National Energy Act.

1979 Jimmy meets with the shah of Iran when he visits Washington, DC.

There is a revolt in Iran, Egypt and Israel sign a peace treaty, and on November 4 sixty-six Americans are taken hostage in Iran. Jimmy Carter negotiates the release of thirteen black and female hostages on November 17.

1980 Jimmy runs for a second term. Iraq invades Iran as Jimmy works to negotiate the release of the remaining fifty-three hostages without giving in to all demands. Jimmy debates Ronald Reagan, the Republican candidate for president. Ronald Reagan defeats Jimmy in the general election, 51 percent to 41 percent.

1981 The hostages are released moments after Ronald Reagan takes office as president. The Carters return to Plains, Georgia, and host the Egyptian president and Israeli prime minister there.

1982 The Carters found the Carter Center. Jimmy begins teaching at Emory University.

1984 Jimmy and Rosalynn volunteer at a Habitat for Humanity project in New York City. They go on to build thousands of homes and become the organization's most popular and famous volunteers.

1987 In Atlanta, the Jimmy Carter Presidential Library and Museum opens.

1998 Jimmy Carter receives his first United Nations Human Rights Prize.

2002 Jimmy Carter is awarded the Nobel Peace Prize. He continues to publish books and go on book tours.

2015 Jimmy Carter celebrates his ninety-first birthday, remains the head of Carter Center, and teaches Sunday school in Plains, Georgia. His good work continues.

CARTER for PRESIDENT

BIBLIOGRAPHY

Carter, Jimmy. *Always a Reckoning and Other Poems*. New York: Times Books, 1995.

———. *Beyond the White House: Waging Peace, Fighting Disease, Building Hope*. New York, Simon & Schuster, 2007.

———. *Christmas in Plains: Memories*. New York: Simon & Schuster, 2001.

———. *An Hour before Daylight: Memories of a Rural Boyhood*. New York: Simon & Schuster, 2001.

———. *Keeping Faith: Memoirs of a President*. Fayetteville, AR: University of Arkansas Press, 1982.

———. *Living Faith*. New York: Three Rivers Press, 2001.

———. *Talking Peace: A Vision for the Next Generation*. New York: Dutton, 1993.

Raum, Elizabeth. *Gift of Peace: The Jimmy Carter Story*. Grand Rapids: Zonderkidz, 2011.

ONLINE RESOURCES

Websites

Jimmy Carter Educational Information, https://jimmycarter.info

Jimmy Carter's Boyhood Home, www.exploregeorgia.org/listing/2697-jimmy-carter-boyhood-home

Education Resources at Carter Library, www.jimmycarterlibrary.gov/education/resources.phtml

The White House Biography of Jimmy Carter, www.whitehouse.gov/1600/presidents/jimmycarter

Videos

Jimmy Carter's Presidential Inaugural Ceremony, https://youtu.be/ifmaoLJTNrk

President Carter at Ninety, in conversation with Thom Hartman about Carter's book *A Full Life: Reflections at Ninety*, https://youtu.be/ksPJ_xISegc

Jimmy Carter's 2005 TED Talk, "Why I Believe the Mistreatment of Women Is the Number One Human Rights Abuse," https://youtu.be/wfW3aZCFfLA

Jimmy Carter's Crisis of Confidence speech: July 5, 1979, https://www.youtube.com/watch?v=1IlRVy7oZ58

"From Peanut Farmer to President," short Jimmy Carter biography, https://youtu.be/UHgz3B70AOg